ART for ALL

Colour In
Art

Elizabeth Newbery

Chrysalis Children's Books

First published in Great Britain in 2001 by
Ⓒ Chrysalis Children's Books
An imprint of Chrysalis Books Group Plc
The Chrysalis Building, Bramley Rd, London W10 6SP
Paperback edition first published in 2004

Copyright © Chrysalis Books Group Plc 2001
Concept and text copyright © Elizabeth Newbery 2001

Editors: Claire Edwards, Kate Phelps
Designer: Jane Horne
Picture researcher: Diana Morris
Consultant: Erika Langmuir
Education consultant: Sue Lacey

ISBN 1 84138 306 6 (hb)
ISBN 1 84138 854 8 (pb)
British Library Cataloguing-in-Publication Data for
this book is available from the British Library.

Printed in Hong Kong
10 9 8 7 6 5 4 3 2 1 (hb)
10 9 8 7 6 5 4 3 2 1 (pb)

Picture acknowledgements
Cover:
The Horniman Public Museum, London: front cover br. Rudolph Staechlin
Family Foundation, Basel/Bridgeman Art Library: front cover c.
Stockmarket/Corbis: front cover tr. Craig Tuttle/Stockmarket/Corbis: front
cover l. Courtesy of the Trustees of the V&A Museum, London: front cover
cr. Private Collection/Bridgeman Art Library: back cover © Warhol
Foundation/DACS London 2001.
Inside:
Agnew & Sons/Bridgeman Art Library: 15tl. Art Institute of Chicago
/Bridgeman Art Library: 13tr & 13cr detail. Arts Council Collection,
Hayward Gallery, London/Bridgeman Art Library: 18b © the artist.
Arts Council of Great Britain/Bridgeman Art Library: 17bl © the artist.
Birmingham Museum & Art Gallery/Bridgeman Art Library: 7tl.
Bury Art Gallery & Museum: 15bl © DACS London 2001. C/B
Productions/Stockmarket/Corbis: 5t. Christies Images/Bridgeman Art
Library: 2, 23cl © DACS London 2001. Collection of 3i plc/Bridgeman Art
Library: 13bl © the artist. Gallerie Daniel Malingue, Paris/Bridgeman Art
Library: 20b © DACS London 2001. Photo David Heald © Solomon R

Guggenheim Foundation, New York: 21tr © DACS London 2001. Hermitage,
St Petersburg/Bridgeman Art Library: 11tl. Hermitage St
Petersburg/Bridgeman Art Library: 18br © Les Hériteurs Matisse. The
Horniman Public Museum, London: 22c & b, 28tr. India Office
Library/Bridgeman Art Library: 23tl. Bob Krist/Stockmarket/Corbis: 5cr.
Hervé Lewandowski/RMN: 7r & 7bl detail. © ADAGP-DACS London 2001.
Louvre, Paris/Giraudon/Bridgeman Art Library: 14. Musée des Beaux Arts,
Nantes/Giraudon/Bridgeman Art Library: 11cr. Courtesy Museum of Fine
Arts Boston. © 2000 All rights reserved. Henry Lillie Pierce Fund 1899: 16.
Photograph © 2001 The Museum of Modern Art, New York: 9br © DACS
London 2001. Acquisition confirmed in 1999 by agreement with the Estate of
Kazimir Malevich and made possible with funds from the Mrs John Hay
Whitney Bequest (by exchange). National Gallery, London/Bridgeman Art
Library: 3, 25bl. National Gallery, Oslo/Bridgeman Art Library: 27t © DACS
London 2001. Osterreichische Galerie, Vienna/Bridgeman Art Library: 25tl,
25cr detail. Clayton J Price/Stockmarket/Corbis: 6. Private
Collection/Bridgeman Art Library: 5br, 8-9, 28bl. Private
Collection/Bridgeman Art Library: 11bl © DACS London 2001. Private
Collection/Bridgeman Art Library: 23br © Warhol Foundation/DACS
London 2001. The Rothko Chapel, Houston/Photo Hickey & Robertson: 9t ©
DACS London 2001. San Vitale, Ravenna/ Bridgeman Art Library: 24br & c.
Rudolph Staechlin Family Foundation, Basel/Bridgeman Art Library: 26c,
27br. Stockmarket/Corbis: 17tl. Tate Picture Library: 15cr © the artist's
estate, 20-21 © DACS London 2001, 21bl © the artist. Craig
Tuttle/Stockmarket/Corbis: 4. Courtesy of the Trustees of the V&A Museum,
London: 25br. Wallace Collection, London/Bridgeman Art Library: 26b. Peter
Willi/Musée d'Art Moderne, Paris/Bridgeman Art Library: 18-19 © DACS
London 2001. Peter Willi/Musée d'Orsay, Paris/Bridgeman Art Library: 1, 10,
12b, 17tr.
Every attempt has been made to clear copyrights but should there be
inadvertent omissions please apply to the publisher for rectification.

Some of the more unfamiliar words used in this book are explained in the glossary on pages 30 and 31.

Contents

Colour is a vital part of our everyday lives. It helps us to describe who we are and how we feel. It attracts our attention and gives out information. It can even save lives!

Colour

Colour plays an important part in nature. Some birds are brightly coloured to attract a mate. Many animals are coloured to blend in with their surroundings so that their enemies won't see them. Colour gives us information, too. Traffic lights tell us when to stop and go, life jackets are luminous orange so they can be easily spotted. We also use colour all the time in our everyday language. You might describe someone as being 'green with envy'. Artists use colour to express their feelings, create moods and make viewers react in a certain way.

▶ *Colour in nature*
Two hundred years ago, a scientist discovered that flowers are coloured for a purpose and not just to look pretty. This sunflower is brilliant yellow so that it attracts the bees that help to pollinate it.

▼ Colour in advertising

Bright colours – especially red, green and orange – can be seen from a long way off so advertisers use them to attract our attention. Colour helps us to remember particular products too. This red logo is recognized instantly all over the world.

▲ Colours that give meaning

Some colours are special to a particular group of people. These flags display the national colours of different countries. Other colours represent groups or organizations like the Red Cross, important people such as kings and queens or sports teams such as a football team.

matters

▶ Rowing Home by Winslow Homer, 1890

Colour is one of the first things you notice in a painting. What would you remember most about this picture? The boat and its passengers? Or the unexpected way that reds, oranges, yellows and brown are used to paint a picture of water and sky?

Why is a banana yellow? You might think that all objects come with their own colour. In fact, colour comes from light. Colour is what we see when light rays are reflected off an object. Many artists explore how this works in their paintings.

Light and

The scientist Sir Isaac Newton (1642–1727) was the first person to discover that all colour comes from light. He shone a beam of white light through a prism (a wedge-shaped piece of glass). The beam split into seven separate colours. Then he passed these seven colours through a second prism – and they turned back into white light again. It proved Newton's idea that all light is made up of these colours. Later, in the 1800s, a group of artists called the Impressionists became fascinated by colour and light and made their own experiments using paint.

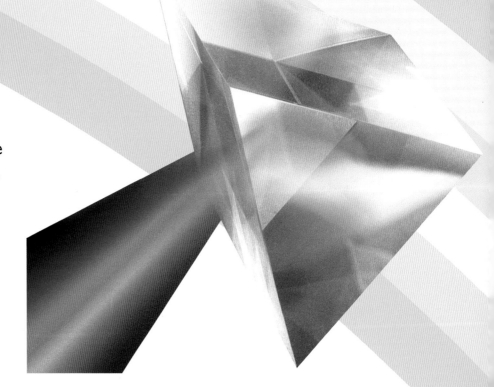

▲ *The colour spectrum*
A beam of light is made up of red, orange, yellow, green, blue, indigo and violet. This range of colours is called the colour spectrum. The colours always appear in the same order. Black and white are not colours so they do not appear as part of the spectrum.

The Blind Girl by
Sir John Everett Millais, 1854–56
Rainbows appear on showery, sunny days because raindrops in the air act like tiny prisms, splitting sunlight into its different colours. In this picture, the artist makes us feel sorry for a blind girl by painting a wonderful double rainbow that she cannot see.

Rouen Cathedral, the West Portal, ▶
Bright Sunlight by Claude Monet, 1894
Claude Monet was one of the greatest Impressionists. He studied how light changed throughout the day, making things look totally different. Monet understood that all light is made up of different colours. Instead of using white paint for bright sunlight, he used tiny marks of the colours in the colour spectrum (see below).

colour

For many centuries, artists have used colour in all kinds of ways. But some artists choose to use black and white instead of colour. Why do they do this?

No colour

Black and white are not really colours because they are not part of the colour spectrum (see page 6). Black is where there is no light – it is the darkest shade. White is the lightest shade, made up of white light (see tone on page 10). Some artists use black and white as though they were colours. Using black or white often has a particular purpose. The writing on signs and in books is usually in black on white so it can be seen or read easily. Silhouettes are pictures made from solid black shapes – no other colour would be as effective. Artists also use black and white to express moods, to create an atmosphere or for special effects.

Silhouette of the Camsie family by ▶
Augustin Edouart, nineteenth century
Silhouettes first became popular in the 1700s. People stood or sat so that a shadow of their profile (side-view) was cast on a wall by candlelight. The outline was traced off and then filled in with black paint or cut out from black card and stuck on a white background.

▶ *The Rothko Chapel, Houston, USA by Mark Rothko, 1967*
Rothko painted 14 pictures for a chapel in America. All of them are in very dark tones and black.
He painted them to create a special atmosphere in the chapel.
Many people find it a very calm place and go there to think quietly about peace and religion.

▼ *Supremist Composition: White on White by Kasimir Malevich, about 1918*
Kasimir Malevich wanted to paint pictures that were separate from nature and which expressed just feelings and nothing more. He painted simple, geometric shapes because they don't exist in nature. He then made the paintings even simpler by taking away any colour.

There is 'tone' in painting just as there is in music. Colour and sound can both be light and dark, heavy and soft and shades of these in between.

Tone control

Tone is the shading of colour from light to dark and all shades of grey in between white and black. Artists use different tones to make a shape look more solid and three-dimensional. They also use it to give a sense of space and distance – to make something look like it is near or far. Like colour, tone may describe the mood, or feelings, the artist is trying to show, such as joy (light tones) or anger (dark tones). It can also give meaning. So light tones are often used to express truth, hope and new life, and dark tones to hint at fear and death. Light tones can suggest goodness and darkness can suggest evil.

▶ *Lion Resting by Rembrandt van Rijn, seventeenth century* In this pen-and-ink drawing, the artist uses just four tones – the black-brown ink at full strength, two tones of watered-down ink and the light-coloured paper. These tell us all we need to know about the shape and texture of the lion.

Woman Combing Her Hair by Edgar Degas, about 1886
Degas was an expert draughtsman (skilled at drawing). He has drawn this picture with softly coloured chalks called pastels. He has used tone to create areas of shadow and light. These make the woman's body seem soft, rounded and full of hollows and dimples.

St Peter's Denial by Georges de la Tour, 1650
In this picture of a Bible story, the artist uses black, dark-brown and red tones for deep shadows. This cleverly suggests secret deals being done in the dead of night. He draws attention to people's faces by showing these highlighted with candlelight, painted in the lightest tones.

Still Life by Giorgio Morandi, about 1952
Almost all of Giorgio Morandi's paintings were simple groups of bottles and bowls, painted in delicate mixtures of colour tones. Here, the objects at the front are not shaded but the different shapes behind them almost look like their shadows. Do you think the effect is slightly mysterious?

Almost all artists use colour in their work. So they learn how to mix it and to understand which colours to put together to get the effect they want.

All mixed up

Red, yellow and blue are called primary, or pure, colours because they cannot be made by mixing two colours together. But any two primary colours can be mixed together to make secondary colours. Equal amounts of red and yellow make orange, of blue and yellow make green and of red and blue make purple. If you use unequal amounts of colour you get intermediate (in-between) colours. For instance, more yellow than red makes yellowy-orange. Mixing more than two colours makes a muddy brown.

▶ *Bedroom at Arles,*
by Vincent van Gogh, 1889
Van Gogh was one of the first artists to understand how colour can be used to express moods such as pain, heartache and joy. Here he has made the white furniture yellowy-orange to give a warm, sunny feeling.

◀ Colour wheel

This colour wheel shows the three primary colours (red, yellow and blue) and the secondary colours that are made by mixing equal amounts of them (orange, purple and green). Colours opposite each other on the colour wheel are called complementary colours. If placed side by side these colours become extra bright. If you stare at them long enough the colours start to flicker.

▲ Sunday Afternoon on the Island of La Grande Jatte by George Seurat, 1884–86

Colour doesn't have to be pre-mixed on a palette – it can be 'mixed' by our eyes and brain. In this painting, Georges Seurat, who was especially interested in colour, put dots of unmixed colours next to each other. For example, the orange parasol is actually made up of tiny blobs of red and yellow (see the close up of the parasol). From a distance, it looks orange.

▲ Midsummer by Bridget Riley, about 1985

Look hard at this painting. Does it appear to jump and flicker? This painting uses complementary colours to create special optical effects. The colours were mixed very carefully – not any old red, green, orange and blue would work. The pattern was measured and drawn very accurately and then painted in by hand. If the artist hadn't worked in this way the optical effects wouldn't have worked so well.

In the past, artists used colour to make people, landscapes and objects look as real and as lifelike as possible. Today, many artists still like to use colour in this way.

Looking

About 600 years ago, oil paints became popular with artists. Unlike other paints in use at that time, oils could be easily smoothed and blended to make things look more real. Artists built up colours in thin layers to trap light and to make them glow and shine. In this way, artists could paint surfaces or textures that looked as if they would actually feel hard, soft, rough or silky. Oil paints also enabled artists to make gradual changes in colour and tone to give a greater feeling of space and distance.

The Virgin of the Rocks by ▶
Leonardo da Vinci, about 1508
Leonardo da Vinci and other artists at that time noted that warm, bright colours such as red stand out and cool, light colours such as pale-blue fall back. They noticed that colours became bluer in the far distance. They used this knowledge to give a sense of space in their paintings.

Still Life with a Basket of Wild Strawberries by Luis Meléndez, eighteenth century

Luis Meléndez painted still-life pictures of everyday objects and food. Notice how he has used colour to make the strawberries look very real. They look so convincing, we can imagine what they taste like.

real

Inland Australia by Sidney Nolan, 1950

Notice how the artist has created the feeling of great distance in this painting. Look how he has used pale-blues in the far distance and strong red in the foreground.

Mother and child by Mark Le Claire, 1980

After photography was invented in 1826, cameras could record what artists had tried to do in the past. So from then on, many painters became less interested in making things look real. Recently, though, some artists have made paintings that look more real than photographs. This painting fools almost everyone into thinking it is a photograph!

Red, orange and yellow are called warm colours because they make us think of fire, the sun and blood. We all know the phrase 'red-hot'. Blue, green and grey are known as cold or cool colours because they remind us of water and shade.

Hot and

Warm colours make us feel happy and excited. Red, the hottest colour, can also make us feel alarmed. All over the world, signs that mean 'Danger!' are painted in red. Cold colours can make people feel calm, thoughtful or sad. They are also linked to keeping clean and healthy. In England, in the eighteenth century, kitchens were painted green or blue because people believed it helped to keep flies away! Even today, a lot of soaps and medicines have blue or green packaging.

▲ *The Slave Ship by Joseph William Mallord Turner, 1840*
Here, hot colours represent a real, bloody deed which happened in 1783. The captain of a slave ship threw 122 dead and dying slaves overboard so that he could claim the insurance money.

Valentine's Day heart

In many countries, red hearts represent love and romance. It is traditional to send cards with pictures of red hearts to loved ones on St Valentine's Day (14 February).

▲ *Portrait of the Artist's Mother by James Abbott McNeill Whistler, 1871*
Whistler has painted this picture in cold, dark colours such as black, white and greeny-grey. His mother wears a plain black dress and stares straight ahead. Do you think her son is showing her in a thoughtful mood? Or does he see her as an old woman, waiting for the end of her life?

cold

◄ *California Seascape by David Hockney, 1968*
This picture uses mainly cool colours, but the painting is not as cold as the one of Whistler's mother. The artist has included warmer colours that make quite a bit of difference. What feelings do the colours in this picture give you?

Colour is not always used to make something look real. All kinds of artists use colours to describe their feelings and express themselves. Sometimes artists break all the rules to experiment with colour as the mood takes them.

Wild about

From the late 1800s and early 1900s, artists were becoming especially interested in colour. Scientists were making new discoveries about colour, and paint was being made with new materials that produced a wider range of shades. Artists started to try out bold new ideas. One group of artists used bright, strong, pure colours instead of creating lifelike pictures with light and dark tones. People were so shocked to see these artists' paintings, they called the group Les Fauves (wild beasts).

The Port of Collioure by André Derain, 1905
This painting was shown at the Les Fauves exhibition in 1905 that had shocked many of the visitors. Later, André Derain said, 'We were always wielding colour like sticks of dynamite. We were always intoxicated [drunk] with colour, with words that speak of colour.' Do you think that people would still find this painting shocking today?

colour

Foy Nissen's Bombay
by Sir Howard Hodgkin, 1975–77
Howard Hodgkin paints pictures of visits to friends and places, meetings and even arguments.
He uses colour as a way of remembering how he felt on these occasions.

Portrait of Madame Matisse
by Henri Matisse, 1913
Henri Matisse experimented with colour all his life.
He said, 'When I paint green it doesn't mean grass; when I paint blue it doesn't mean sky.'
Here, Matisse has used blue-greys to paint his wife's face, neck and hands.

You know that colour can look realistic or can express feelings. But did you know some artists think that colour looks like sound? Or helps people to think?

Just

Some artists think that colour has special meanings or uses. The Russian artist Wassily Kandinsky was interested in colour and sound. Other artists wanted to explore colour just for itself. These artists thought the best way to separate colour from feelings or other meanings was to get rid of brushstrokes and any other signs of an artist at work. Instead, they coloured huge canvases by pouring paint on, staining with colour or putting paint on with a roller.

◀ *Watercolour with a Red Stain by Wassily Kandinsky, 1911* Wassily Kandinsky was interested in colour and sound. He thought light-blue struck the same note as a flute, mid-blue as a cello, dark-blue as a double bass, mid-green as a violin and red as a trumpet. If you could 'listen' to this painting, what sort of sounds do you think you would you hear?

◀ *IKB 79 by Yves Klein, 1959*

When people looked at this picture, the artist, Yves Klein, wanted them to imagine they were looking into nothingness, a bit like outer space. He mixed an especially brilliant blue which he called International Klein Blue (IKB). He thought that if people stared into the big block of blue long enough, it would help them to clear their minds and think more clearly.

Canal ▶

by Helen Frankenthaler, 1963

Helen Frankenthaler used giant untreated canvases to paint on. (Artists usually seal canvas with glue and special white paint called primer so the paint won't soak in.) She laid the canvases on the floor and washed thin layers of colour over them or used colour to stain them.

colour

◀ *As if to Celebrate, I Discovered a Mountain Blooming with Red Flowers by Anish Kapoor, 1981*

Anish Kapoor is a sculptor. He loves the strong colours that he saw in India, where he grew up. Sometimes he covers shapes with deep-coloured powdered pigment to look as though they have grown like that.

For centuries, certain colours have been used to convey special messages about people's culture, traditions and religions. Artists everywhere have shown this in their work. Some artists even give their own meanings to colours.

Coloured

Certain colours are linked to everyday events such as birth, marriage and death. The colours used for these depend on where you live. For example, in Europe and America black is linked with death and white is worn by brides and so is linked with weddings. In some Asian countries, white is the colour of death and red represents marriage. The same object in the same country can give out different messages depending on its colour.

▶ *Devil mask from Bolivia, South America, twentieth century*
The red-and-yellow markings on this mask represent the Devil. Bolivians believe that the Devil watches over their tin mines. Although the mines have brought money to the country, they have also brought misfortune.

Hindu wedding ceremony, artist unknown, about 1887
This Hindu Indian bride is shown wearing the traditional red wedding sari. Many Asian brides still wear red today.

messages

Composition in Red, Blue and Yellow by Piet Mondrian, twentieth century
Here Mondrian uses a horizontal and vertical grid and the primary paint colours red, blue and yellow to represent his ideas. He was a member of a group of Dutch artists called De Stijl (The Style). This group wanted art to show the order, balance and harmony in the world.

Campbell Soup Cans by Andy Warhol, 1965
Warhol was a Pop Artist. His art reflected the bold images of everyday life found in magazines, advertisements and packaging. This work of art represents a brand image (like the one of Coca-Cola on page 5). He has played around with the image by changing the colours of the tins.

Today, people all over the world treat gold and silver as valuable colours. But did you know that purple and yellow were once thought precious, and deep blue was worth more than gold?

Costly colour

The Ancient Romans used a special purple dye made from shellfish found in the Mediterranean Sea. It was so costly to produce that only Roman rulers were allowed to wear it. Since then, purple has been associated with royalty and the Church. In China, only emperors were allowed to wear a light-yellow colour called Imperial Yellow. In Europe during the Middle Ages, a blue mineral called lapis lazuli was ground up to make a deep-blue paint called ultramarine. It was very rare and so expensive that it was only used in the most important part of paintings.

▶ *Empress Theodora and her court, a mosaic from the church of San Vitale, Ravenna, Italy, about AD 47*
A mosaic is a picture made of small pieces of materials, such as marble, set into cement. This one is made of glass, marble, mother-of-pearl, gold and precious stones. Imagine the effect as it gleamed and glittered inside the dark church, lit only by flickering candlelight.

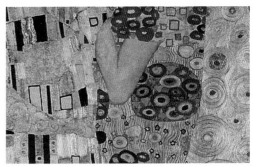

The Kiss
by Gustav Klimt, 1907–8
Gustav Klimt was deeply impressed by the mosaics at Ravenna (see page 24). He often decorated his own paintings with real gold, gold paint and with sequins stuck on to imitate precious stones. What do you think makes this picture look like a mosaic (see detail below)?

▲ *The Wilton Diptych, artist unknown, about 1395*
King Richard II (kneeling, left) ruled England from 1377 to 1399. The artist used lots of gold and ultramarine (see page 24) – the two most expensive materials at that time. The gold shows off Richard's royalty and the precious blue is used to show the saints and angels in heaven.

Porcelain stem pot, Ming Dynasty, early fifteenth century
This Chinese pot is decorated with a beautiful deep-red glaze. The Chinese thought that it was a very special colour – perhaps because it was difficult to make. Pots and dishes decorated with it were placed on altars and used to make offerings to the gods.

Painters depend on good light to see colour. In some places, the light is especially clear and artists may travel long distances to paint there. Other artists like to paint in hot climates, where places are usually more colourful.

Painters and places

Venice in northern Italy is one of the most beautiful cities in the world. In the past, many artists were attracted to the clear light that bounces off the water of its canals and lights up the buildings. Countries in the far north such as Norway and Scotland have more hours of summer daylight than countries farther south. During summer, the light seems especially bright and appears to make colours look stronger.

◀ *Summer Night*
by Harald Sohlberg, 1899
Norway is sometimes called the land of the midnight sun. Harald Sohlberg painted this picture from the balcony of his house overlooking a fjord. Notice how the colour of the flowers and the mountains seem stronger and more intense. The sky seems to glow with a special, magical light.

▶ *Nafea Faa Ipoipo*
(when will you marry?)
by Paul Gauguin, 1892
For the last ten years of his life, Gauguin lived in Tahiti, a Pacific island. In this picture he has painted two women wearing colourful, traditional dress set against the tropical landscape.

◀ *The Bacino di S Marco*
from S Giorgio Maggiore
by Giovanni Antonio
Canaletto, 1724–30
Canaletto was very skilled at capturing the clear bright light in Venice. Notice how he has painted the golden stone buildings and pavements and the water as though they were lit by unseen spotlights.

About the artists

▶ *Giovanni Antonio Canaletto* was born in Venice, Italy, in 1697 and died in 1768. He sold many of his paintings of Venice to tourists and made a lot of money.

▶ *Edgar Degas* was born in Paris, France, in 1834 and died in 1917. He was very interested in photography and liked to paint 'snapshots' of people taking part in everyday activities.

▶ *André Derain* was born in Chatou, France, in 1880 and died in 1954. He was one of the most important of Les Fauves.

▶ *Helen Frankenthaler* was born in New York, USA, in 1928. She developed her own style of painting called 'stain-soak'.

▶ *Paul Gauguin* was born in Paris, France, in 1848 and died in 1903. Gauguin left France for Tahiti, where he died in poverty.

▶ *Vincent van Gogh* was born in Zundert, the Netherlands, in 1853 and died in 1890. During his lifetime most people thought Van Gogh's paintings were worthless. Today they are some of the most valuable paintings in the world.

▶ *David Hockney* was born in Bradford, England, in 1937 but now lives mainly in the USA. Like Degas, he is an expert draughtsman (skilled at drawing).

▶ *Howard Hodgkin* was born in London, England, in 1932. He often takes many years to finish a picture.

▶ *Winslow Homer* was born in Boston, USA, in 1836 and died in 1910. He is best known for his paintings of the sea.

▶ *Wassily Kandinsky* was born in Moscow, Russia, in 1866 and died in 1944. He was fascinated by the connection between colour and music.

▶ *Anish Kapoor* is a sculptor who was born in Bombay, India, in 1954. He is interested in the similarities and differences between Eastern and Western art.

▶ *Yves Klein* was born in Nice, France, in 1928 and died in 1962. He made paintings in all sorts of unusual ways including burning holes in canvases.

▶ *Gustav Klimt* was born in Baumgarten, Austria, in 1862 and died in 1918. He painted pictures of rather cruel-looking women.

▶ *Georges de La Tour* was born in Vic-sur-Seille in France in 1593

and died in 1652. He painted scenes of everyday life and religious paintings.

> *Mark Le Claire* was born in Peterborough, England, in 1951. He is interested in the effect that photography has had on our lives.

> *Leonardo da Vinci* was born in Vinci, Italy, in 1452 and died in 1519. He was a sculptor, writer, architect, inventor, scientist and musician as well as a painter.

> *Kasimir Malevich* was born in Kiev, Ukraine, in 1878 and died in 1935. He is most famous for his works of art called *Black Square* (1915) and *White on White*.

> *Henri Matisse* was born in Le Cateau-Cambrésis, France, in 1869 and died in 1954. Many people think he and Picasso were the two greatest painters of the twentieth century.

> *Luis Meléndez* was born in Naples, Italy, in 1716 (although his parents were Spanish) and died in 1780. He was one of the most talented painters of his time.

> *Sir John Everett Millais* was born in Southampton, England, in 1829 and died in 1896. He was a member of the Pre-Raphaelite Brotherhood who painted pictures with Christian messages.

> *Piet Mondrian* was born in Amersfoort in the Netherlands in 1872 and died in 1944. In 1917, he co-founded De Stijl, a group of artists and designers who made posters, packaging, furniture, architecture and works of art.

> *Claude Monet* was born in Paris, France, in 1840 and died in 1926. He was one of the Impressionists.

> *Giorgio Morandi* was born in Bologna, Italy, in 1890 and died in 1964. He liked to draw the same subject over and over again.

> *Sir Sidney Nolan* was born in Melbourne, Australia, in 1917 and died in 1992. He was one of the first Pop artists as well as being well known for his paintings about Australia.

> *Rembrandt van Rijn* was born in Leyden, the Netherlands, in 1606 and died in 1669. He was one of the greatest artists of all time.

> *Bridget Riley* was born in London, England, in 1931. She is best known for Op Art – paintings that appear to flicker.

> *Mark Rothko* was born in Dvinsk, Russia, in 1903 and died in 1970. He is best known for his paintings of rectangular shapes built up in thin washes of colours very close in tone.

> *Georges Seurat* was born in Paris, France, in 1859 and died in 1891. He invented the technique of painting in dots of complementary colours.

> *Harald Sohlberg* was born in Christiania (now called Oslo), Norway, in 1869 and died in 1955. He was mainly a landscape painter, best known for his pictures of the mountains in central Norway.

> *Joseph Mallord William Turner* was born in London, England, in 1775 and died in 1851. *The Slave Ship* was painted a few years after slavery was finally banned in Britain in 1834, but it was still legal in many countries.

> *Andy Warhol* was born in Pittsburgh, USA, in 1928 and died in 1987. He is one of the best known American Pop Artists.

> *James Abbott McNeill Whistler* was born in Lowell, USA, in 1834 and died in 1903. He was very interested in art and music.

Things to do

Colourful language *pages 4–5*
Make a list of everyday expressions that use colour to describe feelings. Here is one to get you started: 'blue with cold'.

Spot the colour *pages 4–5*
Spot how many things you can see in your local high street that use colour to give information or help you to recognize them. For example, letter boxes are red so they can be seen easily from a distance.

Light into colour *pages 6–7*
You will need a hosepipe. On a bright sunny day, with the sun behind you, take a garden hose. Turn the hose full on then put your thumb over the end of the hose to make a spray. As the drops fall through the air, the light from the sun should catch them and separate into the colours of the spectrum, making a rainbow.

Mixing colour *pages 12–13*
You will need a circle of card measuring about 70 mm across, string about 140 cm long, paints in two primary colours and a sharp point. Divide the circle into six equal segments on both sides of the card. Paint the segments in alternate primary colours. With the sharp point pierce two holes through the centre of the card. Thread the string through the holes and tie the ends together and pull the string taut. Spin the card and pull the string hard to make it go faster.

Glossary

advertising Words and pictures that try to persuade you to buy something.

canvas A type of coarse cloth that artists use to paint on.

cold or cool colours Blue, green and grey.

colour spectrum Red, orange, yellow, green, blue, indigo and violet.

complementary colours Opposite colours on the colour wheel (see page 12): red and green, blue and orange, yellow and purple.

culture Shared ideas and traditions among a group of people.

De Stijl A group of artists, designers and architects who worked together in the Netherlands from 1917 to the early 1930s. They used primary colours and geometric shapes to express the idea of order and harmony in the world.

diptych A painting with two parts, usually hinged together like a book.

fjord A long narrow strip of sea between steep cliffs.

Impressionist One of a group of artists working in the second half of the nineteenth century. They used quick daubs of paint to capture fleeting light or a passing moment. They were seen as revolutionary and were very unpopular with many people.

intermediate colours Colours in between primary and secondary colours, for example yellowy-orange.

lapis lazuli A rare mineral found mainly in Afghanistan. In the Middle Ages it was ground up to make ultramarine, a strong blue paint.

Les Fauves A group of artists who liked to use joyful, strong colours and big brush strokes.

logo A design made to represent a product or company.

luminous colours Colours that glow in the dark.

mood A state of mind or feeling, such as joy, peace, pain, anger or sadness.

mosaic A picture made up of tiny pieces of stone, clay, glass or marble fixed in cement.

mother-of-pearl The lining inside oyster shells and some other shells used to make semi-precious jewellery and decoration.

Op Art Art based on optical effects made to trick the eye.

palette A piece of board on which artists mix their colours.

pastels A type of soft chalk.

pigment The colour in paint.

pollinate Transferring pollen from one part of a flower to another.

Pop Art Art about modern life. It often uses images from comic strips, shopping and advertising.

precious stones Natural rocks that have a high value, such as diamonds.

primary Pure colours that cannot be made by mixing two colours together: red, yellow and blue.

prism A wedge-shaped piece of glass.

secondary Colours that are made by mixing any two primary colours together: orange, green and purple.

semi-precious stones Natural rocks, such as turquoise, that have a high value but not as high as precious stones, such as diamonds.

shade A colour can be dark, light or anything in between. Black is the darkest shade and white is the lightest shade. Examples of shades of colour are dark-blue, mid-green and light-red.

still life A painting of objects and food.

three-dimensional (3-D) A solid shape that has length, width and depth.

tone Shades of colour from light to dark, or all shades of grey in between black and white.

tradition Customs and beliefs handed down from one generation to another.

two-dimensional (2-D) A flat shape that has length and width but no depth.

warm or hot colours Red, orange and yellow.

Index